A PET WHAT?!

MY PET HEDGEHOG

BY PAIGE V. POLINSKY

EPIC

BELLWETHER MEDIA • MINNEAPOLIS, MN

Action and adventure collide in EPIC.
Plunge into a universe of powerful beasts, hair-raising tales, and high-speed excitement. Astonishing explorations await. Can you handle it?

This edition first published in 2020 by Bellwether Media, Inc.

Library of Congress Cataloging-in-Publication Data

Names: Polinsky, Paige V., author.
Title: My pet hedgehog / Paige V. Polinsky.
Description: Minneapolis, MN : Bellwether Media, 2020. | Series: A pet what?! | Includes bibliographical references and index. | Audience: Ages 7-12. | Audience: Grades 4-6. | Summary: "Engaging images accompany information about pet hedgehogs. The combination of high-interest subject matter and light text is intended for students in grades 2 through 7"– Provided by publisher.
Identifiers: LCCN 2019034526 (print) | LCCN 2019034527 (ebook) | ISBN 9781644871829 (library binding) | ISBN 9781618918680 (ebook)
Subjects: LCSH: Hedgehogs as pets–Juvenile literature. | Hedgehogs–Juvenile literature.
Classification: LCC SF459.H43 P65 2020 (print) | LCC SF459.H43 (ebook) | DDC 636.933/22–dc23
LC record available at https://lccn.loc.gov/2019034526
LC ebook record available at https://lccn.loc.gov/2019034527

Editor: Betsy Rathburn Designer: Josh Brink

Printed in the United States of America, North Mankato, MN.

TABLE OF CONTENTS

PRICKLY PALS

A hedgehog smells the air with its long, pointy nose. Then a door slams. The surprised critter curls into a **prickly** ball.

Hedgehogs are small, shy **mammals**.
These popular pets are often called hedgies.

Hedgies have furry faces and bellies. Their tails are short and stubby. But hedgies are known for their long **spines**!

The spines usually lie flat against hedgehogs' bodies. But the spines poke out when the animals curl up!

SO MANY SPINES

Hedgehogs have up to 7,000 spines! They feel like the spines on a hairbrush.

HEDGEHOG PROFILE

- **Animal Type:** mammal
- **Life Span:** 4 to 6 years
- **Length:** up to 8 inches (20 centimeters)
- **Weight:** up to 1 pound (0.5 kilograms)

Wild hedgehogs live in Asia, Europe, and Africa. African pygmy hedgehogs are the most popular hedgehog pets.

COLORFUL CRITTERS

Pet hedgehogs come in 92 different colors! White spines with brown or black stripes are common.

African pygmy hedgehog

Pet hedgies can carry human illnesses. They are **illegal** in some places. In others, they are found through **breeders** or **animal shelters**.

HUNGRY HEDGIES!

Hedgies love to roam! They need large cages with smooth floors and soft **bedding**.

Most hedgies are messy. They use their bedding as a bathroom. But some learn to use **litter pans**. These must be cleaned each day. The rest of the cage should be scrubbed weekly.

bedding

HEDGEHOG CAGE

Hedgehogs are **sensitive** to cold. Heating pads keep their cages toasty.

Hedgies like to live alone in their cozy homes. They hide in soft bedding. Small huts are nice, too!

HEDGEHOG CARE DUTIES

Daily

- ☑ feed
- ☑ change water
- ☑ change bedding
- ☑ bond outside of cage

Weekly

- ☑ scrub cage

As Needed

- ☑ bathe
- ☑ trim nails
- ☑ bring to vet

Hedgies love to eat! Most are fed dry hedgehog food. Live worms and crickets are special treats.

Hedgies should always have fresh water. But they only need two meals a day. Eating too much may cause **obesity**.

FRESH AND FIT

Exercise and healthy food keep hedgehogs fit. Warm homes are also a must. Cold hedgies may **hibernate** and become ill.

Hedgehogs rarely need baths. Owners should gently rub their spines with a soft brush. Nail trims are also important!

HEDGEHOG HEALTH SUPPLIES

nail clippers

baby shampoo

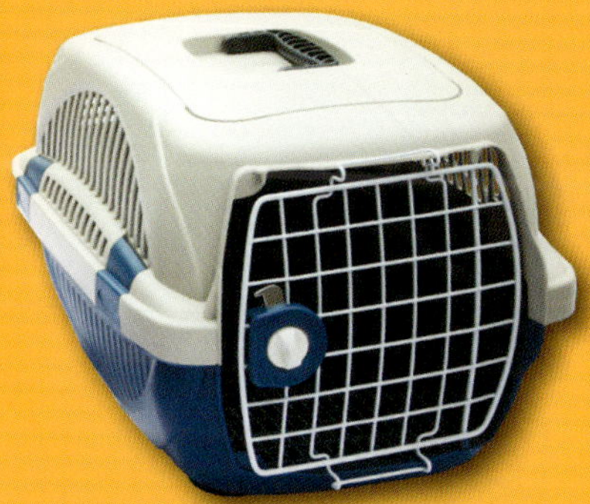

travel carrier
for vet visits

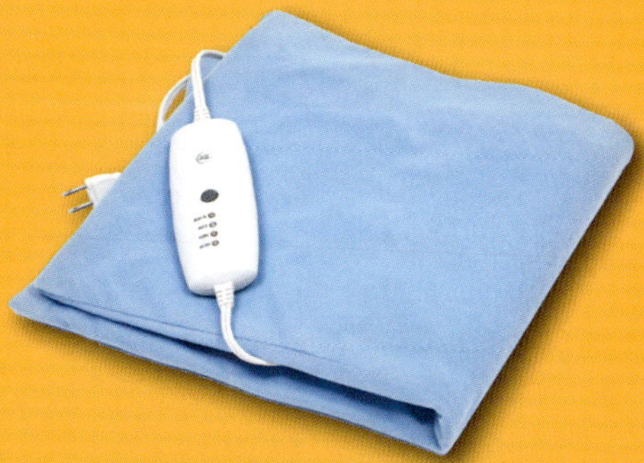

heating pad

toothbrush

Hedgehogs are **nocturnal**. They love to run and play at night.

It takes time and treats for these shy pets to **bond**. Owners must hold and talk to their hedgies daily.

Hedgehogs are **foragers**. They enjoy searching for hidden treats. They also like dragging small toys around.

TINY TUBERS

Hedgies often walk around with empty toilet paper tubes on their heads. Owners call this tubing!

Hedgehogs are prickly. But they are sweet little pets!

GLOSSARY

animal shelters—places that take in animals whose owners cannot care for them

bedding—a soft material used to line animal cages

bond—to form a close friendship with someone

breeders—people who keep and take care of animals to produce more

foragers—animals that go out and search for food

hibernate—to sleep and rest until winter is over

illegal—not allowed by the law

litter pans—pans filled with dry material used as indoor toilets for animals

mammals—warm-blooded animals that have backbones and feed their young milk

nocturnal—active at night

obesity—an unhealthy state of being overweight

prickly—having many sharp points

sensitive—easily hurt or upset

spines—sharp, pointed parts on an animal

TO LEARN MORE

AT THE LIBRARY

Matzke, Ann. *Hedgehog.* Vero Beach, Fla.: Rourke Educational Media, 2015.

Shofner, Melissa Raé. *Hedgehogs.* New York, N.Y.: PowerKids Press, 2018.

Wilson, Paula M. *Hedgehogs.* North Mankato, Minn.: Capstone Press, 2019.

ON THE WEB

FACTSURFER

Factsurfer.com gives you a safe, fun way to find more information.

1. Go to www.factsurfer.com.

2. Enter "hedgehogs" into the search box and click 🔍.

3. Select your book cover to see a list of related web sites.

INDEX

The images in this book are reproduced through the courtesy of: Eric Isselee, front cover (hero); Phonix_a Pk.sarote, front cover (small hedgehog); ohenze, front cover (background); DioGen, pp. 2-3; Best dog photo, pp. 4, 11 (top, bottom, cage interior), 14, 18; NATAYO, p. 5; Thanisnan Sukprasert, p. 6; Csanad Kiss, p. 7; Evgeniia Litovchenko, p. 8; Elijus3000, p. 9; Carmelka, p. 10; maxim ibragimov, p. 11 (cage); Hurst Photo, p. 11 (water bottle); Olga Popova, p. 11 (heating pad); Nicole Mulstay, p. 12; Jenn Huls, p. 13 (top); ALIAKSANDR PALCHEUSKI, p. 13 (bottom); Bennian, p. 15; Jiraporn Thongchai, p. 16; terekhov igor, p. 17 (top left); Bulltus_casso, p. 17 (middle left); New Africa, p. 17 (bottom); Raihana Asral, p. 17 (top right); bjphotographs, p. 17 (middle right); nupook538, p. 19; f.ield of vision, p. 20; Maximilian100, p. 21; bluehand, p. 22.